**Edition Schott**

*Saxophone*

Bernhard Heiden
1910 – 2000

# Sonata

for Alto Saxophone in E♭ and Piano
für Altsaxophon in Es und Klavier

**ED 11195**
ISMN 979-0-2201-0871-6

## Alto Saxophone in E♭

www.schott-music.com

Mainz · London · Berlin · Madrid · New York · Paris · Prague · Tokyo · Toronto
© 1943 SCHOTT MUSIC Ltd, London · Printed in Germany

*For Larry Teal*

# SONATA

**Saxophone in E♭**

BERNHARD HEIDEN (1937)

## I

Saxophone in E♭

# II

## III

# Saxophone in E♭

Schott Music Ltd, London  S&Co.6395